I Am Confident Beautiful and Unique.

I am more than ENOUGH.

Jackie Cantoni

Published by Realizing Dreams

Punta Gorda, Florida

ISBN 978-0-9903128-8-8

Library of Congress Control Number: 2020921631

To every young girl and woman – as you look in the mirror **choose** to see your beauty and uniqueness.

Every girl deserves to grow into
a woman of confidence and self-beauty.

Jackie Cantoni

CONTENTS

Bonus "Me Time" Activities to Flourish & Thrive

Jackie Cantoni

I Am Enough...

I Am Enough...

Do you want to let your light shine? How about radiate with confidence when you walk into a room?

Believing in yourself is the secret to a happier life.

My hope is these pages will awaken your inner beauty, as you fill your mind with positivity.

Have fun as you open this book and absorb the confidence generating I am . . . energy. Re-create your self-belief through your power within.

I am confident you will be even happier.

Jackie Cantoni

My Daily
Positive
Self-Affirmations

I am Confident, Beautiful, and Unique

Stop, pause...What makes you light and breezy?

Face it girlfriend, your outlook on life often stems from the words you are thinking or how you are perceiving yourself in that moment.

How often do you have negative thoughts, often the same ones, repeating over in your mind? This negative self-chatter must be replaced with new positive self-talk. You can only hold one thought at a time. You choose.

These pages of positive self-talk when repeated daily can create courage and a light breezy heart to carry you through.

The power of these simple self-affirmations can transform your negative self-talk to positive self-belief. Sift out the bad. Keep all the good.

Each day apply yourself ... to be your best self.

Whether you are retired, a working mom, entering college, or in middle or high school your happiness is created by your self-confidence. By reflecting on these pages, you can now create confidence in seconds!

This is a personal take-action journal to **"place on your nightstand by your bed and love being you book."** It is a companion book to glance inside of before you go to bed and peek inside of when you wake in the morning. Recharge your thoughts with positive self-talk. The power of positive thinking can skyrocket your happiness.

Believing in yourself can start today. For 14 days, repeat or say out loud each affirmation (or pick one affirmation theme a day) to create a new daily habit mindset. Think about some of the ways you can genuinely live these "I am" affirmations.

Breathe. Take a moment to stop and really reflect on each positive statement. Then sit back and watch how these powerful little words can change your outlook on life, health, wealth, relationships, and self-love.

Are You Ready???

Drum roll please....

Your self-affirmations begin on the next page.

You'll see there is plenty of space for your written thoughts and reflection.

My hope is you have fun journaling on these pages and enjoy the positive outcomes as they manifest in your life. 😊

Jackie Cantoni

I AM

Enough

I AM

Brilliant

Jackie Cantoni

I AM

Strong

I AM

Capable

I AM

Beautiful

I AM
Kind

Jackie Cantoni

I AM

Authentic

I AM
Genuine

Jackie Cantoni

I AM

Compassionate

I AM

Smart

I AM

Bold

I AM

Caring

Jackie Cantoni

I AM

Full of Love

I AM

Passionate

I AM
a Shining Star

I AM

a Bright Light

Jackie Cantoni

I AM

a Masterpiece

I AM

a Work in Progress

Jackie Cantoni

I AM

a Friend

I AM

Self-Confident

I AM

Playful

I AM

Purposeful

Jackie Cantoni

I AM
Driven

I AM

TALENTED

I AM

a Priority

The best investment I will ever make is in myself.

I AM

Dedicated

I AM
Reliable

I AM

FABULOUS

Jackie Cantoni

I AM

Worthy

I AM

Healthy

I AM

ReSiLieNt

I AM

Powerful

Jackie Cantoni

I AM

Gracious

I AM

Stylish

Jackie Cantoni

I AM

Happier

I AM

Inspired

Jackie Cantoni

I AM
Peaceful

I AM

WELL-SPOKEN

Jackie Cantoni

I AM
a Role Model

I AM

Positive

Jackie Cantoni

I AM

Grateful

I AM

Motivated

Jackie Cantoni

I AM

DESERVING

I AM

Unique

I AM
More Than ENOUGH . . .

I AM

THE END

AND YOUR NEW BEGINNING

Are You Ready for More?

Here are a few bonus
"Me Time" Activities to help you

Flourish & Thrive

- Why I love being ME
- My Gratitude Journal
- 21 Days – I am Choosing
- I am a Priority
- I Love My Uniqueness
- I am Deserving, I am Worthy
- Release the Worry
- Share Your Bright Light
- Share Your Smile

Jackie Cantoni

I am Confident, Beautiful, and Unique

Why I love being ME ...

What do you love about yourself?

What is your best feature inside and out?

Create confidence by reminding yourself of your strengths and uniqueness. Confidence and inner beauty grow from knowing and loving the best parts of you. It is then, that you realize the sum of all your parts is the best!

Why I love being me . . .

_____

_____

_____

_____

_____

_____

_____

_____

_____

_____

_____

_____

57

Jackie Cantoni

My Gratitude Journal

Create a positive attitude with 30 days of gratitude

Gratitude is the key that opens the door to a happier life. What we focus on, we become.

Get an appreciative zip in your step and start each day by listing three things you are thankful for. It will put a smile on your face and love in your heart!

Day 1:

1. _____
2. _____
3. _____

Day 2:

1. _____
2. _____
3. _____

Day 3:

    1. _____
    2. _____
    3. _____

Day 4:

    1. _____
    2. _____
    3. _____

Day 5:

    1. _____
    2. _____
    3. _____

Day 6:

    1. _____
    2. _____
    3. _____

Day 7:

    1. _____
    2. _____
    3. _____

I am Confident, Beautiful, and Unique

Day 8:

1. _____
2. _____
3. _____

Day 9:

1. _____
2. _____
3. _____

Day 10:

1. _____
2. _____
3. _____

Day 11:

1. _____
2. _____
3. _____

Day 12:

1. _____
2. _____
3. _____

Day 13:

    1. _____
    2. _____
    3. _____

Day 14:

    1. _____
    2. _____
    3. _____

Day 15:

    1. _____
    2. _____
    3. _____

Day 16:

    1. _____
    2. _____
    3. _____

Day 17:

    1. _____
    2. _____
    3. _____

I am Confident, Beautiful, and Unique

Day 18:

1. _____
2. _____
3. _____

Day 19:

1. _____
2. _____
3. _____

Day 20:

1. _____
2. _____
3. _____

Day 21:

1. _____
2. _____
3. _____

Day 22:

1. _____
2. _____
3. _____

Jackie Cantoni

Day 23:

    1. _____

    2. _____

    3. _____

Day 24:

    1. _____

    2. _____

    3. _____

Day 25:

    1. _____

    2. _____

    3. _____

Day 26:

    1. _____

    2. _____

    3. _____

Day 27:

    1. _____

    2. _____

    3. _____

I am Confident, Beautiful, and Unique

Day 28:

1. _____
2. _____
3. _____

Day 29:

1. _____
2. _____
3. _____

Day 30:

1. _____
2. _____
3. _____

🌿 Gratefulness Reminder

Refer to your gratitude journal to carry you through on days when you need an uplifting boost!

Jackie Cantoni

21 Days – I Am Choosing Challenge

Let the world know You Rock!

Take this challenge whether you want to eat healthier, reconnect with a friend, go for a promotion, start your own podcast, or realize other dreams on your mind and in your heart.

For the next 21 days focus on you. Each day stretch your goals, thoughts, and activities to become your best self. It will be a quick 21 days to form a personal-growth habit and new lifestyle.

After all, isn't life really about realizing dreams?

1. Today I choose to: _____

2. Today I choose to: _____

3. Today I choose to: _____

4. Today I choose to: _____

5. Today I choose to: _____

6. Today I choose to: _____

7. Today I choose to: _____

8. Today I choose to: _____

9. Today I choose to: _____

10. Today I choose to: _____

11. Today I choose to: _____

12. Today I choose to: _____

13. Today I choose to _____

14. Today I choose to: _____

15. Today I choose to: _____

16. Today I choose to: _____

17. Today I choose to: _____

18. Today I choose to: _____

I am Confident, Beautiful, and Unique

19. Today I choose to: _____

20. Today I choose to: _____

21. Today I choose to: _____

One step at a time. One choice at a time.

Are you ready for your 21 new choices to boost your self-worth and create confidence? Are you ready to realize a new, bold dream?

During the next 21 days, step back and see how your happiness grows.

Jackie Cantoni

I am a Priority

How often do you sink to the bottom of your "to do" list caring for others? Whether you choose to face it or not, you are subconsciously deflating your own value as you slide down in importance.

Let's make you a priority!!! No excuses. Shift your thinking and write your name at the top of your daily list. You know deep down when you take care of yourself you can better love and care for those around you. Including yourself.

Self-care leads to confidence and positive energy. I am confident you will be even happier. Your happiness will radiate in other areas of your life — making friends, loving your family, advancing your personal and professional success, and realizing your dreams.

Jot down an overdue self-care activity you will do to nurture your soul. I moved myself up and now start my day with an energizing walk. Do you. Have fun and do what you love. Making yourself a priority is lifechanging!

_____

_____

_____

Jackie Cantoni

I am Confident, Beautiful, and Unique

I Love My Uniqueness

You deserve the best life has to offer. This starts with a healthy self-worth.

What secret special essence makes you ... you? What do you have that is unique to you? Confidence and self-love come from accepting who you are and appreciating every inch of yourself.

Think about your traits. Which ones make you unique and special? There is only one answer...every single fiber of your being is special. Every first and last trait makes you fabulous, unique, and unconditionally beautiful.

These beliefs are thoughts that begin in your mind. Self-love is a mindset shift.

Through positive self-affirmations, knowing why you love yourself, taking care of yourself, being thankful, and embracing the power of choice – you can overflow with self-love and self-confidence.

Whisper to yourself, "I love and appreciate my uniqueness". Steve Jobs, Founder of Apple, once shared it is not about being better, it is about being different.

Your difference is your strength. Your uniqueness is what makes you powerful, deserving, and special.

Now it's your turn.

Five traits that make me unique and beautiful are:
(write five unique traits here that capture you)

Separate out any bad habits, which are not necessarily character traits. Through your positive voice, action steps, and accountability, you can one day at a time reverse and replace these negative habits. The first step starts with positive self-talk to further create belief in yourself.

Each day boost your happiness and well-being as you remind yourself why you love and are thankful for your unique self. Smile as you soak-in these five **being-you** traits.

Celebrate your uniqueness!

I am Confident, Beautiful, and Unique

Jackie Cantoni

"Do something nice for yourself."

I am Deserving
I am Worthy

Hey girlfriends, what is up with the guilt? Why as women do we often feel we are not worthy or deserving? Why do guys tend to not feel this?

We may not have the courage to ask for something because we are afraid of the answer or do not believe we are deserving. We live this lack of worthiness in work, around the house, having fun, making moments for ourselves, or pursing a little or really big dream. It is time for us to overcome this guilt and skyrocket our happiness.

Picture your dream life. Where are you? Who are you with? What are your surroundings? Release the guilt and know you deserve a happy life. You are worthy of friendships, confidence, self-care, accomplishments, and much more.

Muster up your courage, as it is time to re-build from years of negative self-talk. Step into a life of joy starting with fresh, encouraging words that you can repeat to yourself.

You may be stuck...and not even realize your thoughts are influencing your behavior. For example:

Old Negative Thought:

I have always been the cute, chubby girl.

New Positive Thought:

I am deserving of being fit, trim, and healthy.

I choose to put more focus and effort into my life.

Visualize one of your biggest goals or dreams and draw it here:

Bubble up all your energy and jot down at least three steps to achieve your goal and realize your dream:

_____

_____

_____

_____

_____

I am Confident, Beautiful, and Unique

Now that you have written the getting started steps, let's cement them one step at a time. Schedule your first action step on your calendar. You are deserving and worthy of achieving your goal and realizing your dream.

These two powerful words – deserving and worthy - can unpack old baggage and replace it with newfound motivation.

Whisper to yourself or yell out loud, "I am deserving", "I am worthy". Repeat this daily. We believe what we hear over and over.

For years you have convinced yourself of a thought pattern that is now your current mindset. This is only a thought pattern. With the power of this book and positive thinking, you can create a new, bold habit to manifest an abundant life overflowing with confidence and self-love.

God wants you to be deserving, worthy, and abundant. God made you unique. Your unique gifts and best self can change your life and you can change the world.

Jackie Cantoni

Release the Worry

Do you at times feel you have the weight of the world on your shoulders? This mindset of worry can take your energy and hold back your dreams.

Are you ready to feel lighter, breezier, and radiate with confidence?

The best strategy for releasing worry from your life is to focus on the moment. It is an extremely simple lesson yet how often are we not present in the moment? Our thoughts and negative self-chatter are filled with worry about what happened yesterday and what tomorrow will bring.

There is a difference between planning and worrying. How often do you fill your mind with non-present thoughts? Are you saying to yourself it is most of your day? Worry and negative thoughts weigh us down, sucking the energy and life right from under us.

Ladies, take your energy back!

To release the worry, replace it with the positive self-affirmations you learned in this book. Refill your mind with positive, freeing thoughts to create an even happier attitude. The re-energized you will love your daily moments and your life.

Jackie Cantoni

*"I've come to believe that each of us
has a personal calling
that's as unique as a fingerprint."*
— Oprah Winfrey

Now it is your time to shine:

Remember, be kind to yourself...
- You are a masterpiece.
- You are more than enough.
- You are beautiful and unique.
- You've Got This!

Reveal yourself as a masterpiece. You are beautiful, unique, and talented. At the same time, know the best version of you will not always be perfect. And that is okay. Life is not perfect. Yet, as a work in progress, you are still fabulous. Do not let time slip away waiting for perfection.

83

Jackie Cantoni

Spread Your Bright Light . . .

*"One of the hardest things in life
is to be brave enough to be yourself."*
- Lady Gaga

Discover what you love and reveal it to the world.

In a world often filled with negativity, refill your mind with positivity. It is simple and powerful. The first step toward your dream life can be the most frightening. Self-doubt is more likely to squash more hopes than failure. Remove self-sabotage and replace negative thoughts with positive affirmations. Just as you breathe, whisper your *I Am* . . . sayings throughout your day – while driving, walking from your car, in the shower, cooking breakfast, brushing your teeth . . . creating a new energized, fun you.

Do you often get stuck in the mode of comparing yourself to others? Let go of the anxiety of viewing other's "perfect lives" and "perfect on-line accomplishments". For one day, put yourself first and focus on creating your confidence and pause scrolling through other's on-line posts. Quiet your mind to hear what is in your heart. Disconnect from your devices and reconnect with yourself. Choose to enjoy your time spreading your light. Let your bright light shine.

Afterword

Be Sure to Pass on Your Uniqueness to Others

Share Your Smile . . .

Are you ready to help spark the light for a friend, mom, sister, or daughter to realize her unique value?

It is your turn to pass on your uniqueness as a gift to the world.

> *"When you smile at someone,*
> *if they do not smile back,*
> *then they needed your smile more than you."*
> - Jackie Cantoni

One of the best gifts you can give to others is confidence. Confidence to believe in themselves, to appreciate the value they bring to the world, to pursue their passions and strive to live their best life.

As we come to a close, I hope you see this in yourself - you are confident, beautiful, and unique. You are more than ENOUGH. Your smile and uniqueness can change the world.

I am Confident, Beautiful, and Unique

One person at a time, share YOU and your smile. Pass on your confidence, beauty, and uniqueness to others!

Do you. Be you.

I Am
Confident
Beautiful
and Unique.

I am more than ENOUGH.

*Join us for girlfriend chats and
confidence creating activities at
www.areyoureadybook.com*

About the Author

Jackie Cantoni is founder of *The Best You*™ program,

an award-winning mentor, author, and dynamic speaker who shares key strategies and transformational lessons to live a happier life.

Jackie is author of *"Are You Ready? A Guide to Be the Best Version of You"*. In all her works, Jackie instills an unwavering self-belief, so you are inspired to see it in yourself.

Jackie loves coaching for personal and professional growth and mentoring students to nail their job interviews and kick-start career success.

Jackie has two sons and lives in Florida with her husband, Jim Cantoni author of *"7 Steps for Empowering Youth: Self-Awareness Developing Grit and a Growth Mindset"*. Together they have authored two children's books, *"I Love You, Two™"* and *"Give a Hug . . . Get a Hug™"*.

"Me Time" activities include biking, swimming, golf, long walks, the beach, and spending quality time with family and friends.

Jackie Cantoni

My Notes:

I am Confident, Beautiful, and Unique

My Notes:

Jackie Cantoni

My Notes:

I am Confident, Beautiful, and Unique

My Notes:

Jackie Cantoni

My Notes:

I am Confident, Beautiful, and Unique

My Notes: